Christian Stegerer, Stefan Risse

Benchmarking of Java Cryptoalgorithms

A comparison of different algorithms in different java libraries

GRIN Verlag

Bibliografische Information der Deutschen Nationalbibliothek:

Die Deutsche Bibliothek verzeichnet diese Publikation in der Deutschen National-
bibliografie; detaillierte bibliografische Daten sind im Internet über http://dnb.d-
nb.de/ abrufbar.

Dieses Werk sowie alle darin enthaltenen einzelnen Beiträge und Abbildungen
sind urheberrechtlich geschützt. Jede Verwertung, die nicht ausdrücklich vom
Urheberrechtsschutz zugelassen ist, bedarf der vorherigen Zustimmung des Verla-
ges. Das gilt insbesondere für Vervielfältigungen, Bearbeitungen, Übersetzungen,
Mikroverfilmungen, Auswertungen durch Datenbanken und für die Einspeicherung
und Verarbeitung in elektronische Systeme. Alle Rechte, auch die des auszugsweisen
Nachdrucks, der fotomechanischen Wiedergabe (einschließlich Mikrokopie) sowie
der Auswertung durch Datenbanken oder ähnliche Einrichtungen, vorbehalten.

Imprint:

Copyright © 2008 GRIN Verlag GmbH
Druck und Bindung: Books on Demand GmbH, Norderstedt Germany
ISBN: 978-3-640-31845-2

This book at GRIN:

http://www.grin.com/en/e-book/126115/benchmarking-of-java-cryptoalgorithms

GRIN - Your knowledge has value

Der GRIN Verlag publiziert seit 1998 wissenschaftliche Arbeiten von Studenten, Hochschullehrern und anderen Akademikern als eBook und gedrucktes Buch. Die Verlagswebsite www.grin.com ist die ideale Plattform zur Veröffentlichung von Hausarbeiten, Abschlussarbeiten, wissenschaftlichen Aufsätzen, Dissertationen und Fachbüchern.

Visit us on the internet:

http://www.grin.com/

http://www.facebook.com/grincom

http://www.twitter.com/grin_com

Benchmarking of Cryptoalgorithms

Stefan Risse, Christian Stegerer

Scope

Do a comparison of current cryptoalgorithms and cryptolibraries. Find a benchmarking concept and do the benchmarking.

Abstract

Cryptographic algorithms have nowadays serious impact on many fields of modern life. A good example is the SSL technology, that consists of both symmetric as well as asymmetric cryptography. It is used in thousands of websites like online banking websites to secure transfered data. For the developers of such applications the performance of employing cryptography may be a crucial factor to the success of the complete product. Normally a software developer utilizes cryptographic operations by the usage of precast cryptographic libraries. Therefore, it is interesting to analyze the speed of cryptographic libraries which implement abstract cryptographic algorithms. In the following, we describe our benchmarking of various cryptoalgorithms in different cryptolibraries in different languages on a 32-bit system. In the first part, we outline our preparatory work and our considerations on setting up a fitting benchmarking environment. With this test environment we conducted the benchmarking of seven JAVA cryptolibraries, namely SUN-JCE, Flexiprovider, Bouncy Castle, Cryptix Crypto, IAIK-JCE, GNU crypto and RSA JSafe. Additionally, we benchmarked RSA BSafe, a cryptographic library, which is written in C++, to isolate the influence of the JAVA virtual machine abstraction layer on cryptographic performance. In the second part, we present a condensed illustration of the benchmarking results and our interpretation, for symmetric cryptography, asymmetric cryptography, the generation of hash based massage authentication codes and digital signatures. These results reveal remarkable differences in speed between the algorithms as well as between the different implementations. Also the choice of the underlying operating system has influence on the execution speed of the cryptographic code. In this work we demonstrated that software developers could gain a multiple of the execution speed of the cryptography utilizing parts of their programs just by a wise selection of cryptographic algorithms and libraries. Furthermore our work can help as a guideline for developing a generic benchmarking model for cryptoalgorithms.

Contents

List of Figures

List of Tables

1 Introduction

1.1 Objectives of this paper

Cryptoalgorithms are intensivly used in different fields of computing. Examples are: the creation of checksums of documents on the internet using trap door hash functions, the encryption of hard disks in public administration to secure data with symmetric encryption, or the use of digital signatures and asymmetric cryptography in business communication. Everybody who uses cryptoalgorithms in software development may ask themselves which algorithm or library is best for their project. In order to provide some help on this decision we measured a certain selection of cryptoalgorithms of nearly all available java crypto libraries with regards to performance. Moreover we chose to use the latest Windows operation system Vista and a up-to-date Linux distribution to find out if the choice of the operation system has influence on the performance of the algorithms. Although the performance measuring is our main approach, we want to present in our spadework how long algorithms with respect to their key lengths should be used in order to guarantee security. Finally, we compare the benchmarking results of the JAVA libraries to the benchmarking results of RSA BSsafe, a C++ library, to provide a relation between java byte code and native machine code of C++. This comparison is of special interest, because RSA provided us with the same library for JAVA (namly JSafe) and C++ (namely BSafe) and therefore one can directly compare the isolated influence of the programming language on cryptographic performance.

1.2 Related work

A measurement of cryptoalgorithms has been performed by various groups in the past. NIST(National Institute of Standards and Technology) as a non-regulatory federal agency within the U.S. Department of Commerce wanted to look for a new standard algorithm for symmetric encryption in 1997 (see [13]). Of course a part of their selection process was benchmarking performance that included both software and hardware testing. In comparison to our work the number of tested algorithms was limited due to the fact that only symmetric cipher algorithms were benchmarked. ECRYPT (European Network of Excellence for Cryptology) started in November 2004 with a similar approach. The Phase 2 report shows the current progress [8]. The difference was that the objective of ECRYPT was to identify new stream ciphers that might become suitable for widespread adoption. This project is called eSTREAM and is still going on until May 2008 when phase 3 will be finished. The NESSIE project (New European Schemes for Signatures, Integrity and Encryption) is a project within the Information Society Technolgy (IST) Program of the European Commission[6]. The main goal of it was to find a portfolio of strong cryptographic primitives. Performance measuring was also a part of this selection process. All of these described works were examined and are basis of our proceedings.

2 SETUP of Cryptobenchmarking

2.1 Security Levels

At the beginning of our work we allocated the different kinds of crypto algorithms to security levels we defined.

The basis of our security levels are the appraisements of various groups including ECRYPT and NIST which we already mentioned. Additonal BSI (German Federal Office for Information Security) and DCSSI (Central Information Systems Security Division) published recommandations of keylengths to maintain certain periods of secureness. The only scientific work available was done by Lenstra [11]. All of these groups use the key length as an indicator of how long crypto algorithms might be secure in the future including symmetric block ciphers, symmetric stream ciphers, asymmetric cryptography and hash functions. After the evaluation of these papers we defined four security levels similar to the annual report of ECRYPT[4]. The difference of our security levels to those of this European institute is that we only defined 4 levels in comparison to 7 levels of ECRYPT. The reason for that is the weakness of the first two levels, that describe very insecure security levels, which we thought are not applicable nowadays anymore. Additionally, we also ignored the highest security level of ECRYPT because we are of the opinion that security in cryptography cannot be foreseen for more that 30 years (which is already very optimistic). So we defined security equivalents for 2 to 3 years, 10 years, 20 years and 30 years. Based on that we decided not simply to overtake the key length values of ECRYPT, but to evaluate all the recommendations of BSI[2], NIST[7], DCSSI[3], Lenstra[1][11] and also ECRYPT to create a broad basis for our levels. The detailed recommendations can be seen in the appendix. It became clear quickly that these organizations / authors have more or less similar estimations. Only ECRPYT differs significantly for the last security level 4. According to Lenstra the recommended key length for asymmetric encryption should be more than 15000 bits, that is approximately four times the estimations of all the other groups. Moreover we realized that Lenstra has very optimistic estimations in comparison to the other groups. This is understandable when we read Lenstra carefully. Namely he only defines a minimum limit for keylength instead of a real security level. The BSI does not give a prognosis for more than 5 year from now on. Additionally, the draft paper of the BSI only cares about digital signatures, so we couldn't use this for the definitions of our security levels. In order to be prudent we decided to choose the maximum keylength of all these different recommendations for each kind of crypto algorithm except this one case where ECRPYT has very different results. In this case we chose the average of all publications which lead to a key length of 6136 bit for asymmetric cryptography and security level 4.

The defined security levels have two main implications for our work: On the one hand they provide a niveau to compare algorithms which provide different level of security in the same class e.g. MD5 vs. Whirlpool for hashing. On the other hand we wanted to provide an easy way to look up results with regard to the future time frames of security. The complete overview of our defined security levels can be seen in table 1.

	LEVEL 1: SHORT TIME SECURITY (2-3 YEARS)	LEVEL 2: LEGACY STANDARD LEVEL (10 YEARS)	LEVEL 3: SECURE FOR MAX. 20 YEARS	LEVEL 4: SECURE FOR MAX. 30 YEARS
symmetric	80Bit	112Bit (NIST/ECRYPT)	128Bit (ECRYPT)	256Bit (ECRYPT)
asymmetric	1536Bit (DCSSI)	2432Bit (ECRYPT)	4096Bit (DCSSI)	6136Bit (average)
hash function	224Bit (NIST)	256Bit (DCSSI)	256Bit (ECRYPT/DCSSI)	512Bit (ECRYPT)

Table 1: security levels with keylength and recommending institute

SYMMETRIC BLOCK ALGORITHMS	REASON FOR SELECTION
Rijndael (AES), MARS, Serpent, Twofish, RC6	AES Finalists
Misty, Camelia	Recommended by NESSIE
Cast-5/Cast-6, IDEA	used in PGP
3DES and DES, Blowfish	standard

Table 2: overview of the tested symmetric block ciphers

2.2 Selecting the candidates for benchmarking

In the following paragraphs we would like to answer the question: "Which algorithms are to be benchmarked?". We will present the selected algorithms grouped by kind and explain the criteria of our selection procedure. The basis of the algorithm selection was again the recommandations of the various mentioned groups like NIST or ECRYPT. Additionally to their recommendations, we included algorithms that seemed to be interesting for the comparsion results due to their widespread use for example DES for symmetric cryptography or MD5 for the hashing algorithms. Lastly, we also had a look at the candidates of the libaries we wanted to test, to conclude which algorithms are implemented in most of our testing candidates.

The finally choosen algorithms grouped by kind can be seen in tables 2, 3, 4 and 5.

Not shown extra in the tables above but also included in the benchmarking are Message Authentication Codes (MAC), which are based on hash functions. Also not shown above is digital

SYMMETRIC STREAM CIPHERS	REASON FOR SELECTION
RC4	widely used in WLANs for WEP encryption

Table 3: overview of the tested symmetric stream ciphers

ASYMMETRIC ALGORITHMS	REASON FOR SELECTION
RSA	possibly the most used asymmetic crypto algorithm
ElGamal	well known algorithm that uses discret logarithm maths

Table 4: overview of the tested asymmetric ciphers

HASH FUNCTIONS	REASON FOR SELECTION
MD5	not secure anymore but widely used
RipeMD, Tiger	Third Round of ECRYPT
Whirlpool, SHA	Recommended by NESSIE

Table 5: overview of the tested hashfunctions

signature cryptography, which is also based on those hash functions together with asymmetric cryptography.

After the selection of the algorithms the next task was to choose the libaries for testing. In this context we included a comprehensive set of the available libraries for the programming language JAVA. We included the following seven so called JAVA crypto provider, or libraries, to our performance testing:

- **JCE SUN** The security provider of SUN Microsystems is included in JDK. We used version 1.6 which is available from http://java.sun.com

- **Flexiprovider** is developed by the Cryptography and Computer Algebra Research Group of Prof. Dr. Johannes Buchmann at the Departement of Computer Science at Technische Universität Darmstadt; The current version is 1.5p1 available from http://www.flexiprovider.de.

- For **Bouncy Castle** from the group "Legion of BouncyCastle" there are two available versions: a full version and a lightweight one. We tested the full version, which is available in version 1.38 from http://www.bouncycastle.org.

- **Cryptix** from the Cryptix Foundation is tested in snapshot version 20050328. It is available from http://www.cryptix.org.

- **IAIK-JCE** The Stiftung Secure Information and Communication Technologies(SIC), established by the Institute for Applied Information Processing and Communication(IAIK) of the Graz University of Technology is responsible for devoloping this library. We used the version 3.16 available from http://jce.iaik.tugraz.at.

- **GNU Crypto** is part of the GNU project that is maintained by the Free Software Foundation (FSF). For our tests we included verion 2.0.1 from http://www.gnu.org.

- **RSA JSafe** the cryptographic components for JAVA in version 3.6 were provided by RSA the security division of EMC.

COMPONENT	CHARACTERISTIC	COMMENT
CPU	Intel Merom Core 2 Duo T7300 2,0 Ghz	Stepping: E1; Extensions: MMX, SSE, SSE2, SSE3
RAM	2048 MB DDR2 667 Mhz	actual Timings: 5-5-5-15 (CL-RCD-RP-RAS)
Motherboard	Intel Crestline-GM GM965	Intel AGTL+ 64 Bit effective speed 800 MHz

Table 6: hardware specifications

We also included the library BSafe from RSA Security in our performance testing to provide a comparison with a library which is written in C++ and has therefore native machine code performance.

- **RSA BSafe** the cryptographic components for C in version 6.3.2 were provided by RSA the security division of EMC.

2.3 The test environment

After selecting theoretically which algorithms and libraries are to be tested, we had to care about the setup of the testing environment. These considerations involved the hardware as well as the software environment for testing.

2.3.1 Hardware platform

Thinking about the underlying hardware platform for the benchmarks we had to decide how modern the constituating hardware should be. In general it is better to use a more modern personal computer than an older pc, because the results will then be interesting in both regards, in absolute terms as well as relative figures. We must nonetheless admit that the absolute figures are going to be outdated in two or more years anyway. For the interpretation of the results the speed of the actual testing hardware is not important because the results are to be read and interpreted relativly to each other. One restriction to this assertion can be added: If the situation eventuates that a newer cpu has special optimizations which are supported by some single libraries (not by all), then this would influence the relative library ranking and therfore be an exception to the rule that "the hardware basis is not important".

Our test system was composed of a intel core 2 duo processor with 2 Ghz clock speed and 2048 MB of 667 Mhz DDR2 RAM sitting on a Intel Crestline-GM 965 Northbridge with a Front Side Bus Speed of 800 Mhz. More detailed information is presented in table 6.

2.3.2 Operating Systems

As well as the influence of the hardware we made some considerations about the underlying operating systems for benchmarking. Our main concern about the operating system was that a modern OS may influence benchmarking metrics through its inherent time sharing mechanisms, mainly by interrupt requests (IRQ) of the kernel to the central processor. The starting point of our thoughts was to use a real-time operating system for benchmarking, in order to get the most accurate results and to minimize the influence of interrupt requests on benchmarking metrics. However we did not have time and money to acquire commercial real-time plugins for Microsoft Windows an Linux. We finally prefered to set up a "real life" testing environment. This lead to a standard installation of the two common up-to-date operating systems: Microsoft Windows Vista and Ubuntu Linux 7.10. Moreover we came to the conclusion that results for standard installations of operating systems may be more interesting than a special testing operating system. In addition we switched off every service of the operating system which could trigger a long lasting kernel interrupt. Here is a short list of the deactivated or not installed services of standard operating system installation:

- Anti-Virus services
- Indexing services
- Task planner services

2.3.3 Software Environment

Additionally to the operating system environment, the software development environment also influences benchmarking metrics. For our JAVA testing the software development environment consists of the "JAVA Development Kit 6 Update 3" with accompanying "JAVA Virtual Machine" from SUN Microsystems and the current releases of the available crypto libraries (see above). To do the JAVA benchmarking we wrote a single JAVA program which makes use of the JAVA Cryptography Architecture (JCA). This feature of the JAVA programming language provides an interface to access all the different crypto libraries via a standardized java interface in the same manner. By the use of the JCA technology it was then possible to integrate every single library into one benchmarking program that handles the complete benchmarking process. In practice there were some libraries that differed slightly from the JCA standard. The GNU crypto library differs significantly from the SUN JCA standard, but our testing program made it possible to implement some extra methods and branches for those special libraries.

For the single C/C++ library BSafe from RSA we chose to use the Microsoft Visual Studio 2005 IDE as the library itself was tested by RSA with that product.

2.4 Performance measuring in modern systems

In modern hardware, different time sources with different qualities for time measuring and software development exist. As to Microsoft, there exist five sources of timing/counting in a modern x86 pc [12]:

- 8254 PIT
- RTC
- APIC Timer
- PM Clock
- High Precision Event Timer
- Time Stamp Counter (TSC): fast, completely unreliable. Frequency changes, CPUs diverge over time.

All these timers have different qualities like resolution, wether the timer is cpu internal or external, etc. Our criteria for a good timer for performance benchmarking are that the timer is highly precise to detect the differences between the runtime of various crypto libraries and secondly that the timer is reliable even when the program is for example switching cores in our dual core processor. The advantage of the timer selection procedure was that when coding a benchmarking program you do not have to care in low-level programming about the appropriate timing source. All we had to do is find out which method of the coding language gives us the best timer with regards to our criteria.

For JAVA it is very easy to find a timer which matches our criteria, because of the:

```
1 System.nanoTime();
```

method, which offers the feasibility to make use of the most precise timer on a very abstract level. This means that the method is independent of the operating system and can thus be used under Windows and Linux for high precision timing because it automatically returns the most precise timer available on the system. It is recommend for benchmarking by the "Software Design and Quality Institute" of the University of Karlsruhe[15] as a first choice. We also evaluated other possibilties for benchmarking in JAVA for example the hrlib-library which was developed by Vladimir Roubtsov [14]. However none of the evaluated possiblities offers more ease or precision than "System.nanoTime()".

For C/C++ you have to differentiate between Windows and Linux operating system because the abstraction layer of the JAVA runtime environment is missing and thus you have to use the most appropriate timing source depending on the API of the operating system. We made test runs with every provided method and chose the best one. For the Microsoft Windows operating system we identified the "QueryPerformanceCounter" method of the Windows API as the most exact and suitable method for our benchmarking.

2.5 The bench code for JAVA

The provided abstraction layer made it relativly easy to use the different crypto libraries. A so-called "provider" that is responsible for the matching between the defined standard and the intern functions has to be installed the following way:

Listing 1: register Security Provider

```
1    Security.addProvider(new packagepath.ProviderConstuctor());
```

This approach offers a standardized way to access all cryptographic operations of all the different libraries. The relevant part of the benchmarking core of our program written in pseudo JAVA looks like this:

Listing 2: Time Measuring

```
1    long minTime = Long.MAX_VALUE;
2    long maxTime = 0;
3    long sum = 0;
4    int zaehler = 0;
5    while(true){
6            long start = System.nanoTime();
7            cipherobject.init();
8            cipherobject.doMainCipherOperation();
9            long end = System.nanoTime();
10           sum += (end-start);
11           zaehler++;
12           if((zaehler >= MAX_RUNS) && (sum >= MAX_RUNTIME) break;
13   }
14   writeMeasuringToFile();
```

For our benchmarking we took the current time in nanoseconds before and after the main crypto operation call including its initialization. In a first version of the benchmarking program we measured, in addition to the average runtime, the minimum and maximum runtime of the cryptographic operation. When we analysed the output later we found that the maximum runtime of an algorithm did not make much sense in our results, because the reason for this maximum lies more or less in the interrupt calls of the kernel and is therefore stochastic with regards to the perspective of our benchmarking program. In a later version we took the measurement of the overall time taken and calculated the average of the overall runtime, because in contrast to the minimum runtime the average represents a more real life performance value. To compensate for the mistakes of measuring times with an interrupting kernel, we did the benchmarking runs of the cryptographic primitives a certain numbers of iterations and caluclated the average time at the end. Our minimum runtimes and iterations for the different cryptographic primitives for JAVA can be seen in table 7.

Statistical deviations were not examined in detail. We desisted from verifing the test results with a t-test or similar statistical methods. Several reason were to be said against it. First, tests showed that there are only slight differences between the single iterations of the benchmark runs. Only a few outliers were found during the runs. They were smoothed out by a minimum number of benchmark iterations for each algorithm and the fact that we always compared the average values. On the other hand the additional work for recording and analysing each result of every iteration would have produced a large amount of data an adding only a minimal advantage for

14

verifing results. More detailed verification may be done by future work and thus is not a part of this work. However, we hold that our results reflect the real speed of the algorithms.

CRYPTOGRAPHIC PRIMITIVE	MINIMUM EXECUTION TIME	MINIMUM ITERATIONS RUNS
symm. encryption/decryption	3s	100
asymm. encryption/decryption	10s	3
hashing and hmac	3s	100
signing and verifying	3s	10

Table 7: iterations for cryptographic operations

The input dimensions to our core for the testing were:

- **Provider** or library
- **Algorithms** as far as supported by a provider
- **Keylengths** to be seen in table 1
- To examine if the **plaintext length** has significant influence on the algorithm speed (length-/time) we created random texts with the lengths: 128kbyte, 256kbyte, 512kbyte, 1mbyte and 2mbyte and ran the benchmarking for every plaintext length. Of course we also verified the correctness of our implementation with encrypted and decrypted text.

3 RESULTS of Cryptobenchmarking

3.1 Results JAVA

In order to give a clear picture of the results we will now only present the key facts, split into the security levels defined at the beginning. In this section we only consider the JAVA language and compare the results for Linux and Windows together. We tested with 5 different input lengths as described above, but in the discussion we will focus on the results of 1 megabyte plaintext length input. The reason for this is that after a review of the output data we detected a linear coherence. That means that for example the encryption of 128 kilobytes lasts half the time of encryption of a file with 256 kilobytes. That does not proove a statistical coherence in general, as we did not use statistical tests. For our interpretation, however, it does not make a difference as our benchmark data behaves as if this coherence was given. First we will present both key setups, symmetric and asymmetric. Then proceed with encryption and decryption for both. This is followed by the digital signing and verifying. In the end we will describe the hashing and generation of hash based message authentication codes.

3.1.1 Key Setup for symmetric cryptography

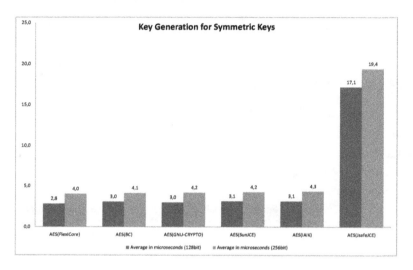

Figure 1: Key Generation for symmetric keys

The core process in symmetric key setup is the generation of a random number. Hence the aim of our testing was to detect whether there are differences in the provided random number generators.

The benchmarking results for key setup for symmetric encryption reveal very short runtimes. All the algorithms need only a range of single-digit to double-digit microseconds to generate a key. Moreover most of the tested key setup algorithms differ here in the range of 300 nanoseconds only. These time intervals and the overall measurement time are very near to our maximal measurement accuracy. Moreover, the symmetric key has only to be generated one time for use. This two factors both reduce the importance of the symmetric key setup speed for choosing a library. Nevertheless we will have look at an exception. The provider JSafe from RSA Security differs remarkable from the other libraries. It is approximately 2 to 3 times slower, especially considering the algorithms RC4, AES and TripleDES. The reason for that is not obvious. There was no possibility to compare the key generation algorithms, as there are only the binaries available from JSafe. A reason for the lower speed might be that the implementation of RSA Security pays more attention to a secure key than the other providers and therefore lasts longer. These differences appear both in Windows and in Linux, but in general these operation systems are not equal. All the algorithms are slightly slower using Linux. This might be a result of using a different kind of random generator in Linux. In figure 1 we only display the AES libraries as an example, because there were no significant differences to the other algorithms.

In conclusion, in this part, it can be stated that symmetric key setup is as fast as expected. Even though there were some runtime differences between the algorithms, we do not think that symmetric key setup has enough importance, in comparison to the other cryptographic operations, to be used as a choosing criteria for an algorithm or a library.

3.1.2 Key Generation for asymmetric cryptography

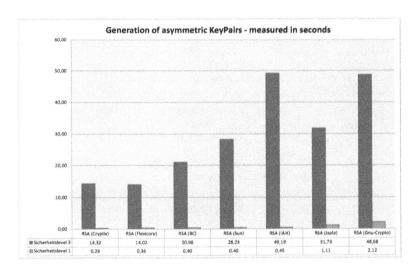

Figure 2: Asymmetric Key Generation

The asymmetric key setup is a more complex cryptographic operation than the generation of symmetric keys. For example for the algorithm RSA, the asymmetric key setup performs the generation of a prime number combination. This calculation is quite difficult to perform.

As described above RSA and ElGamal were the candidates to be tested for asymmetric cryptography. During our first benchmarking runs we were confronted with the problem of extremely long runtimes for the ElGamal key setup, for two of the three supporting libraries. The key setup with ElGamal with the keylength 4096 bit and FlexiCore as the provider lasts for example about four and a half hours. As to time limits we decided not to use ElGamal for our benchmarkings and focused on the comparison of the different providers with the algorithm RSA. ElGamal may be examined in future work by other groups.

The generation of the RSA keys lasts from half a second at security level 1 to around 10 minutes at security level 4. Figure 2 displays the ranking of the provider at security level 1 and security level 3. At security level 1 the fastest provider, Cryptix, is more than eight times faster than the slowest provider, GnuCrypto. This tendency goes on in security level three, but decreases to the factor of three. Also, the ranking of the providers is quite security level comprehensive. The benchmarking under Linux draws a similar picture as under Windows. Especially at security level 1 the differences are marginal. The time interval from the fastest to the slowest implementation within the generation of 4096 bit keys is also equivalent to the Windows results, only the ranking is different. It is mentionable that IAIK's implementation of the RSA key generation is much faster with Linux compared to Windows.

It is very likely that the speed differences are a result of a different security standard concerning the keys. This standard could be independent from the key length. However, that can not be proven here, because it is not within the scope of our paper to examine the quality of the algorithms. In general, the selection of a library, based on the duration of the key generation, is again questionable as the keypair has to be created once only. In our opinion more attention should be given to the performance of encryption and decryption - presented in the following sections.

3.1.3 Symmetric Encryption and Decryption

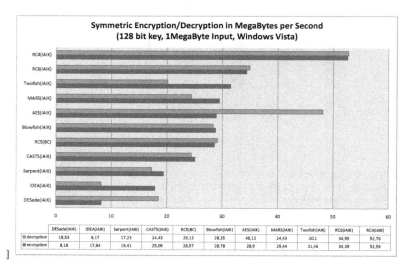

Figure 3: Symmetric Encryption and Decryption using Windows Vista

The data volume of the results for this and the following section are quite large, which is why we present the analysis figures as a ranking of the algorithms in their fastest implementation. As the

18

name implies, symmetric encryption and decryption are symmetric reversing operations, which use for both ways the same cryptographic key. We would thus normally expect the same speed for encryption and decryption.

In this context it seems a bit surprising that some implemented algorithms at operating system Windows Vista encrypt faster than they decrypt, or decrypt faster than they encrypt. For example the encryption of Twofish is nearly 50% faster than its decryption operation and also AES shows great variance here. The deviations between the encryption and decryption runtime do not appear on operating system Linux as can be seen in figure 4. Both operations run at the same speed on Linux. The reason for this behavior is not analyzed here and might be examined in further work.

On the operating system Windows ten out of the twelve tested algorithms were implemented fastest by IAIK-JCE (see figure 3). As described in their product brochure, their implementations were optimized on speed and memory consumption[10]. With regard to performance this is a statement that we can confirm. Only BouncyCastle and CryptixCrypto implemented in each case one algorithm faster. Linux is different, as no library really stands out. Therfore the selection of a library depends on the algorithm which is to be used. All the RC4 implementations are faster than the next fastest algorithm. But we have to take into consideration that this algorithm is a stream cipher. Furthermore, this algorithm is not secure at the present day, as discussed in a lot of papers [9]. Additionally, the Linux benchmarks for RC4 show a runtime, which is at least twice as fast. There might be some optimizations on Linux that can not be used on Windows. For the rest of the tested algorithms one can state that there are slight differences in speed with a linear decrease in rankings, but these differences are small. At the end of our ranking is the algorithm TripleDES, for both Windows and Linux. This is expected as TripleDES is a three time execution of the ageing DES algorithm. All the tested algorithms are considerabl faster on Linux. The AES (for SunJCE) encrypts on average with 41,84 megabytes per second on Linux in comparison to 28,90 megabyte per second using Windows.

For Microsoft Windows the choice of the fastest libraries is predetermined. For Linux the choice of the fastest library is dependent on the algorithm you want to use, because the results for this operating system are quite heterogeneous. Considering the algorithms in general, AES, RC6 and Blowfish may be selected as they are fastest in both encryption and decryption.

3.1.4 Asymmetric Encryption and Decryption

As already mentioned only RSA was tested for asymmetric encryption and decryption.

For encryption most of the results are in the interval of around 90 kb/s for security level 1 and around 230kb/s in security level 3. This figures, which show that all libraries are equally fast, might be a result of the fact that most of the tested libraries have a publicly available source code and it is very likely that the developers incooperated enhancements of other libraries into their own product. The only outlier with regard to asymmetric encryption in the field of the tested libraries is JSafe. The speed of this library is about five times the speed of the other libraries in every security level (see figure 5). A possible explanation for this might be that the library uses some unpublished optimizations . It could also be that the library uses computational tricks,

19

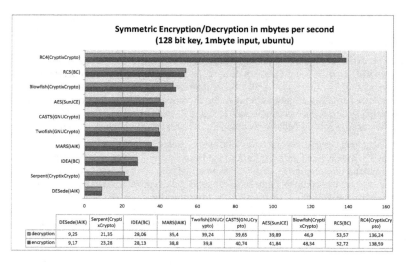

Figure 4: Symmetric Encryption and Decryption using Ubuntu

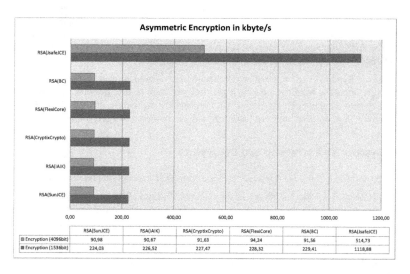

Figure 5: Asymmetric Encryption using Windows Vista

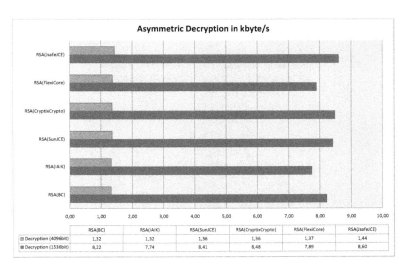

	RSA(BC)	RSA(IAIK)	RSA(SunJCE)	RSA(CryptixCrypto)	RSA(FlexiCore)	RSA(JsafeJCE)
Decryption (4096bit)	1,32	1,32	1,36	1,36	1,37	1,44
Decryption (1536bit)	8,22	7,74	8,41	8,48	7,89	8,60

Figure 6: Asymmetric Decryption using Windows Vista

which might be harmful to security. The true reason for that could only be revealed by a code review in collaboration with RSA Security.

Asymmetric Decryption is on average eleven times slower than the analog encryption operation (see figure 6). In comparison to encryption there are no significant speed differences among the libraries. The difference between the fastest and the slowest libraries is an interval of 10 %. The benchmarking results for asymmetric encryption and decryption on Linux were equivalent to Windows, but only about 30% faster.

As we cannot reveal the true nature of JSafe's success, the figures of this library have to be read carefully. In result the performance values of asymmetric encryption are not a good reason for choosing a certain library. Also the decryption speed differences are too low to draw profound conclusions. All in all we would like to state that within the field of asymmetric RSA cryptography we do not see a performance advantage of a certain library. Therefore the choice in this field has to be made on the basis of other critera than performance.

3.1.5 Hash Generation and MAC Generation with HMac

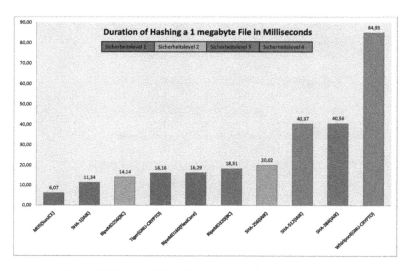

Figure 7: Benchmarking of hash function using Windows Vista

The evaluation of the hashing algorithm implementations brings interesting findings. We would like to mention that in the diagrams the unit of performance is different. We present all the algortihms ranked by the time needed for hashing 1 megabyte input data.

Figure 7 shows the fastest implementation for every tested hash function, with the corresponding provider. Firstly the speed disparity of the different MD5 implementations is appreciable. The duration is in the range of about 6,07 millisecond for SunJCE, the fastest library, to about 10,61ms for BouncyCastle which is for the MD5 the poorest implementation with regard to performance. This significant difference of about 75% speed gain can be achieved just by choosing the right library for a software development project in JAVA, which is in our opinion remarkable. Although we must admit that the use of MD5 for hashing operations is not recommend any more, because in recent history it became possible to compute collisions for this function [5]. Considering all the other hash functions, one can identify significant speed differences among the algorithms. Basically, the execution speed decelerates with increasing hash length. However, there are some exceptions to this rule. Some of the hash functions, like RipeMD256 and SHA-512, offer a high performance, in respect to our security level classification, and can even beat algorithms with shorter hash lengths. Like in symmetric encryption for Windows a single library can convince especially in the SHA implementations. The results in Linux are similar to Windows. The ranking, as it can be seen in figure 8, is the same as in Windows. Furthermore the fast MD5 and SHA1 algorithms are only slighly faster using Linux. A more significant performance difference can be seen when considering the more secure hash functions. The fastest SHA-512 implementation on Linux can beat its Windows counterpart by 15% and Whirlpool even reaches a 30% speed advantage. As a consequence we Linux has advantage over Windows, in case secure hashing has to be done.

Due to the significant speed differences for the algorithms a conclusion can be drawn. In general if security is not of importance and a high performance has to be reached, MD5 might still be a fitting algorithm. In the case of higher security requirements, the algorithm RipeMD320 has a very good security/speed relationship and if long term security is important, SHA-512 is a good choice.

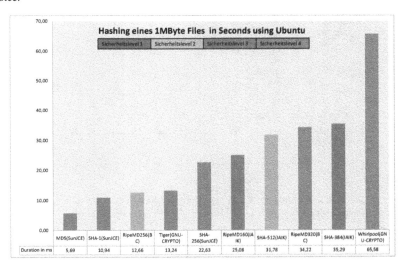

Figure 8: Benchmarking of hash functions using Linux

The MAC generation with hash based message authentication codes is not to be examined in detail here, as the duration of generating a HMac is always equivalent (linear shifted) to the used hash function. It lasts for example 11.34 milliseconds to hash 1Megabyte with the fastest implemented SHA1 algorithm on Windows and 15.96ms to generate the according HMac, which is also the fastest implementation. This evaluation can be considered over all the algorithms and as a consequence the results of the according hash function have to be transfered to the HMac implementations.

3.1.6 Signing and verifying with asymmetric cryptography

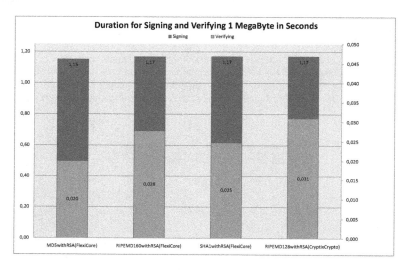

Figure 9: Signing and verifying using Windows Vista: Security Level 4

Digital signatures are a combination of hashing algorithms and asymmetric cryptography. Therefore the results are expected to form a combination of the single performances.

The performance situation in signing and verifying is analog contrary to the situation in asymmetric encryption and decryption, as both operations make use of the RSA algorithm (digital signatures just add a hashing operation to the RSA cryptography). As the signing operation has the lions share of runtime on RSA based cryptography, using the private key of the cryptosystem (analog to asymmetric decrypting) this operation is expected to last much longer than the verifying (using the public key).

This is also affirmed by our results in this section. The signing operation is (almost) equally fast for all the tested signature algorithms. The reason for that lies in the dominance of the RSA based cryptography, which behaves as mentioned above. The verifying operation shows a different picture. The ratio of the RSA algorithm to hashing operation in the verifying is much smaller than in the signing. That is why the differences between the algorithms become evident. The MD5 based algorithm can show a more than 50% better performance than the RipeMD160 based signing algorithm in security level 4 (see figure 9). In comparison to the pure hash functions, the use of MD5 here is not a security risk, as the RSA is executed after the hash value is calculated. Moreover, the reachable security is a combination of the used keylength for the RSA algorithm and the hashlength of the used hash function. The same results can be considered using Linux. Equivalent to hashing und RSA cryptography, benchmarking results are again 30% to 40% faster than the according Windows figures. Our conclusion here is that the use of RSAwithMD5 can be recommended under the precondition that the chosen keylength for the RSA operation is sufficient according to our defined security levels.

3.2 Comparison JAVA to C++

The benchmarking of the BSafe library from RSA Security was done to offer a comparison of the differences between C++ and JAVA performance for the same cryptographic code. This plan is possible as we had the chance to benchmark the two libraries BSafe (C++) and JSafe (JAVA) which are both from the same manufacturer. This circumstance makes it likely that both implementations are similar and allow an appropriate comparison. One restriction we had to acknowledge. An elaborate verification of the C++ runtime results was not possible due to time restrictions. Thus the following findings have to be treated with caution.

The figures 10, 11 and 12 show the symmetric, asymmetric and hashing operations as a comparison between JAVA and C++. In general a clear performance advantage for C++ can be seen here.

The time differences in symmetric cryptography vary very strongly especially at the decryption operations. The reason for these variances lie in the different encryption and decryption speed as discussed in the section "Symmetric Encryption and Decryption" because encryption in C++ is always between 250 and 300% faster than in JAVA. Apart from this, the ranking of the algorithms are the same, which is no surprise, as the algorithms are implemented by the same supplier. The situation in asymmetric operations diverges a little from this. The key setup for security level 1 is only around 6 % faster than in JAVA and 36% faster at security level 3. Otherwise decryption is much faster here, nearly 690% at security level 1. But as mentioned above this results should be treated carfully. Encryption is not discussed here because the deviant results are in JAVA.

Hashing again reveals a fully expected picture. The three considered algorithms MD5, SHA1 and SHA256 all beat their JAVA counterparts clearly, if implemented with C++. The SHA1 algorithm is a especially remarkable, which is 259% faster using C++.

The bottom line here is that the expected considerably time advantage of C++ compared to JAVA is really given. It would be very interesting to compare older tests with our work to find out if JAVA could gain on C++. All in all C++ is still the first choice, if performance is an important factor. It should still kept in mind that a JAVA implementation is much easier and also the threat of commit rough coding errors is smaller.

Comparison Symmetric Algorithms C++ and Java (RSA Security)				
Algorithm	Operation	C++	Java	Difference
3DES	Decryption	17,80	12,02	+48,10%
DES	Decryption	41,39	21,26	+94,69%
AES256	Decryption	67,53	21,33	+216,58%
AES128	Decryption	89,31	53,09	+68,22%
RC4	Decryption	154,39	20,98	+635,88%
3DES	Encryption	17,65	5,03	+250,91%
DES	Encryption	41,27	12,04	+242,76%
AES256	Encryption	65,65	17,81	+268,62%
AES128	Encryption	88,48	20,83	+324,75%
RC4	Encryption	163,63	40,45	+304,53%

Figure 10: Comparison Symmetric Operations C++ and JAVA

	Asymmetric Operations	C++	Java	Difference in %
RSA1536	Key Setup	1,49	1,59	-6,19%
RSA4096	Key Setup	20,06	31,72	-36,76%
RSA1536	Encryption	1336,89	1118,88	+19,48%
RSA4096	Encryption	182,68	514,73	-64,51%
RSA1536	Decryption	68,04	8,6	+691,16%
RSA4096	Decryption	4,88	1,44	+238,74%

Figure 11: Comparison Asymmetric Operations C++ and JAVA

Comparision Java and C++: Hashing 1MB File in Milliseconds			
Algorithm	C++	Java	Difference
SHA256	12,91	23,2	+79,70%
SHA1	4,08	14,66	+259,71%
MD5	2,87	7,28	+153,24%

Figure 12: Comparison Hashing C++ and JAVA

4 Conclusion

It has been found, that there are a many remarkable differences in speed between the algorithms and the different implementations. In some cryptographic operations it becomes really clear which library or algorithm should be used. In other cases it depends on the security level, that is to be reached, as to which algorithm is the right choice. The hash functions belong to this group. Generally it appeared that Linux is the better choice for carrying out cryptography at a high speed. Moreover, our test with the C++ library BSafe form RSA Security discloses that with C++ can still reach a much higher speed than JAVA. The future will show if JAVA catches up with C++.

In future works, an examination of further c/c++ libraries would be very interesting to provide a more deep comparison of the speed differences between different coding languages. Moreover, a generic model for testing and comparing different benchmarking runs over a long time is under discussion as this would give even more objectiv results and also enhance the comparability of the benchmarking runs.

References

[1] Eric R. Verheul Arjen K. Lenstra. Selecting cryptographic key sizes. *Journal of Cryptology: the journal of the International Association for Cryptologic Research*, 14(4):255–293, 2001.

[2] Bundesnetzargentur. Bekanntmachung zur elektronischen signatur nach dem signaturgesetz und der signaturverordnung. Technical report, Bundesnetzargentur, 2007.

[3] DCSSI. Mécanismes cryptographiques. Technical Report Version 1.10, DCSSI, 2006.

[4] ECRYPT. Yearly report on algorithms and keysizes. Technical report, ECRYPT, 2006.

[5] Arjen K. Lenstra et al. Vulnerability of software integrity and code signing applications to chosen-prefix collisions for md5. November 2007. http://www.win.tue.nl/hashclash/SoftIntCodeSign/.

[6] B.Preneel et al. DRAFT final report of european project number ist-1999-12324, named new european schemes for signatures, integrity, and encryption. Springer-Verlang, April 2004. https://www.cosic.esat.kuleuven.be/nessie/.

[7] Elaine Barker et al. Recommendation for key management. Technical report, NIST, 2007.

[8] Steve Babbage et al. Short report on the end of the second phase. eStream, ECRYPT Stream Cipher Project, 2007. http://www.ecrypt.eu.org/stream.

[9] Scott Fluhrer, Itsik Mantin, and Adi Shamir. Weaknesses in the key scheduling algorithm of RC4. *Lecture Notes in Computer Science*, 2259, 2001.

[10] IAIK. Secure information and communication technologies, 2007. http://jce.iaik.tugraz.at/.

[11] Arjen K. Lenstra. Key lengths. In *The Handbook of Information Security*. 2004.

[12] Microsoft. Guidelines for providing multimedia timer support, September 2002. http://www.microsoft.com/whdc/system/CEC/mm-timer.mspx.

[13] NIST. Report on the development of the advanced encryption standard (aes). Technical report, NIST, 2000.

[14] Vladimir Roubtsov. Profiling cpu usage from within a java application, November 2002. http://www.javaworld.com/javaworld/javaqa/2002-11/01-qa-1108-cpu.html.

[15] Rico Starke. Performancemessung, June 2007. http://sdqweb.ipd.uni-karlsruhe.de/wiki/Performance-Messung.

5 Appendix

RECOMMENDATIONS OF KEYLENGTHS

level	secure until	recommended by	algorthm	bitlength
1	2010	Lenstra / Verheul (2004)	sym	75
1	2010	Lenstra / Verheul (2004)	assym	1112
1	2010	Lenstra / Verheul (2004)	Hash	150
1	2010	ECRYPT	sym	80
1	2010	ECRYPT	assym	1248
1	2010	ECRYPT	Hash	160
1	2010	NIST	sym	80
1	2010	NIST	assym	1024
1	2010	NIST	Hash	224
1	2010	DCSSI	sym	80
1	2010	DCSSI	assym	1536
1	2010	DCSSI	Hash	160
2	2017	Lenstra / Verheul (2004)	sym	80
2	2017	Lenstra / Verheul (2004)	assym	1300
2	2017	Lenstra / Verheul (2004)	Hash	159
2	2017	ECRYPT	sym	112
2	2017	ECRYPT	assym	2432
2	2017	ECRYPT	Hash	256
2	2017	ECRYPT	Elliptic Curve	224
2	2017	ECRYPT	Hash	224
2	2017	NIST	sym	112
2	2017	NIST	assym	2048
2	2017	NIST	Hash	224
2	2017	DCSSI	sym	100
2	2017	DCSSI	assym	2048
2	2017	DCSSI	Hash	256

Table 8: Recommandatons for Keylengths in regard to security

3	2027	Lenstra / Verheul (2004)	sym	86
3	2027	Lenstra / Verheul (2004)	assym	1601
3	2027	Lenstra / Verheul (2004)	Hash	171
3	2027	ECRYPT	sym	128
3	2027	ECRYPT	assym	3248
3	2027	ECRYPT	Hash	256
3	2027	NIST	sym	112
3	2027	NIST	assym	2048
3	2027	NIST	Hash	224
3	2027	DCSSI	sym	100
3	2027	DCSSI	assym	4096
3	2027	DCSSI	Hash	256
4	2037	Lenstra / Verheul (2004)	sym	93
4	2037	Lenstra / Verheul (2004)	assym	1939
4	2037	Lenstra / Verheul (2004)	Hash	186
4	2037	ECRYPT	sym	256
4	2037	ECRYPT	assym	15424
4	2037	ECRYPT	Hash	512
4	2037	NIST	sym	128
4	2037	NIST	assym	3072
4	2037	NIST	Hash	256
4	2037	DCSSI	sym	100
4	2037	DCSSI	assym	4096
4	2037	DCSSI	Hash	256

Table 9: Recommandatons for Keylengths in regard to security(2)

WINDOWS RESULTS

Security Level 1	Time in Microseconds	Security Level 2	Time in Microseconds
Blowfish(GNU-CRYPTO)	2,507	Blowfish(GNU-CRYPTO)	2,811
RC4(SunJCE)	2,508	CAST6(BC)	2,833
CAST5(CryptixCrypto)	2,508	Blowfish(SunJCE)	2,844
Blowfish(BC)	2,515	Blowfish(CryptixCrypto)	2,844
Blowfish(SunJCE)	2,516	RC4(SunJCE)	2,859
RC4(GNU-CRYPTO)	2,526	CAST5(CryptixCrypto)	2,865
Blowfish(CryptixCrypto)	2,536	RC4(BC)	2,881
RC4(CryptixCrypto)	2,54	Blowfish(BC)	2,89
CAST6(BC)	2,555	RC4(CryptixCrypto)	2,895
CAST5(BC)	2,567	RC4(GNU-CRYPTO)	2,907
RC4(BC)	2,582	CAST5(GNU-CRYPTO)	2,912
CAST5(GNU-CRYPTO)	2,588	CAST5(BC)	2,914
CAST6(GNU-CRYPTO)	2,617	CAST6(GNU-CRYPTO)	2,96
RC4(IAIK)	2,669	CAST5(IAIK)	3,015
Blowfish(IAIK)	2,676	Blowfish(IAIK)	3,04
CAST5(IAIK)	2,731	RC4(IAIK)	3,081
RC4(JsafeJCE)	16,122	RC4(JsafeJCE)	15,546

Security Level 3	Time in Microseconds		Time in Microseconds
MISTY1(FlexiCore)	2,652	MARS(GNU-CRYPTO)	3,079
MISTY1(GNU-CRYPTO)	2,687	Serpent(BC)	3,083
MARS(FlexiCore)	2,778	CAST5(GNU-CRYPTO)	3,083
IDEA(FlexiCore)	2,782	Serpent(GNU-CRYPTO)	3,09
RC6(FlexiCore)	2,783	RC4(CryptixCrypto)	3,092
AES(FlexiCore)	2,795	RC6(GNU-CRYPTO)	3,095
Serpent(FlexiCore)	2,802	Twofish(BC)	3,103
Twofish(FlexiCore)	2,835	RC6(IAIK)	3,104
CAST5(CryptixCrypto)	2,938	AES(SunJCE)	3,108
AES(GNU-CRYPTO)	2,968	IDEA(GNU-CRYPTO)	3,116
CAST5(BC)	3	AES(IAIK)	3,119
Blowfish(CryptixCrypto)	3,002	Twofish(GNU-CRYPTO)	3,126
Blowfish(GNU-CRYPTO)	3,005	IDEA(BC)	3,145
Rijndael(GNU-CRYPTO)	3,008	Serpent(IAIK)	3,149
CAST6(BC)	3,01	RC4(IAIK)	3,166
Serpent(CryptixCrypto)	3,019	Twofish(IAIK)	3,167
MARS(CryptixCrypto)	3,039	CAST5(IAIK)	3,182
RC4(GNU-CRYPTO)	3,044	IDEA(IAIK)	3,202
Blowfish(BC)	3,047	Blowfish(IAIK)	3,221
AES(BC)	3,049	MARS(IAIK)	3,234
Blowfish(SunJCE)	3,062	DESede(BC)	3,464
Twofish(CryptixCrypto)	3,064	DESede(FlexiCore)	4,317
RC4(BC)	3,066	DESede(IAIK)	5,134
RC6(CryptixCrypto)	3,07	DESede(GNU-CRYPTO)	11,338
CAST6(GNU-CRYPTO)	3,071	AES(JsafeJCE)	17,149
RC6(BC)	3,072	RC4(JsafeJCE)	17,307
RC4(SunJCE)	3,074	DESede(JsafeJCE)	37,713
IDEA(CryptixCrypto)	3,075		

Figure 13: Symmetric Key Setup (1-3) at operating system Windows Vista

31

Security Level 4			
Time in Microseconds			Time in Microseconds
Twofish(FlexiCore)	3,917	AES(GNU-CRYPTO)	4,162
MARS(FlexiCore)	3,956	Serpent(GNU-CRYPTO)	4,162
RC6(FlexiCore)	3,966	CAST6(GNU-CRYPTO)	4,186
AES(FlexiCore)	4,002	MARS(GNU-CRYPTO)	4,186
MARS(CryptixCrypto)	4,008	Twofish(CryptixCrypto)	4,189
Serpent(FlexiCore)	4,025	Serpent(IAIK)	4,208
CAST6(BC)	4,067	RC6(CryptixCrypto)	4,212
Blowfish(BC)	4,069	AES(SunJCE)	4,218
Serpent(CryptixCrypto)	4,07	RC6(GNU-CRYPTO)	4,235
Serpent(BC)	4,092	Twofish(GNU-CRYPTO)	4,256
RC6(BC)	4,094	MARS(IAIK)	4,261
AES(BC)	4,101	Twofish(IAIK)	4,295
Blowfish(CryptixCrypto)	4,104	AES(IAIK)	4,311
Blowfish(SunJCE)	4,126	Blowfish(IAIK)	4,313
Twofish(BC)	4,127	RC6(IAIK)	4,35
Blowfish(GNU-CRYPTO)	4,144	AES(JsafeJCE)	19,368

Figure 14: Symmetric Key Setup(4) at operating system Windows Vista

Asymmetric Key Generation			
Time in Seconds			Time in Seconds
RSA(BC, 1536)	0,934576205	RSA(BC, 4096)	14,3174112
RSA(CryptixCrypto, 1536)	0,77284506	RSA(CryptixCrypto, 4096)	14,0219662
RSA(FlexiCore, 1536)	1,133066136	RSA(FlexiCore, 4096)	20,982583
RSA(GNU-CRYPTO, 1536)	3,603047402	RSA(GNU-CRYPTO, 4096)	28,2259854
RSA(IAIK, 1536)	1,595831523	RSA(IAIK, 4096)	49,1948324
RSA(JsafeJCE, 1536)	1,578583571	RSA(JsafeJCE, 4096)	31,7253823
RSA(SunRsaSign, 1536)	1,158234247	RSA(SunRsaSign, 4096)	48,6825931
RSA(SunRsaSign, 2432)	5,264612495	RSA(SunRsaSign, 6136)	283,956515
RSA(FlexiCore, 2432)	3,050212177	RSA(FlexiCore, 6136)	215,096245
RSA(CryptixCrypto, 2432)	6,00691396	RSA(CryptixCrypto, 6136)	318,58994
RSA(BC, 2432)	11,83908565	RSA(BC, 6136)	61,8863395
RSA(IAIK, 2432)	4,168209716	RSA(IAIK, 6136)	75,3303202
RSA(GNU-CRYPTO, 2432)	10,67481146	RSA(GNU-CRYPTO, 6136)	338,136149

Figure 15: Asymmetric Key Generation at operating system Windows Vista

Symmetric Encryption/Decryption - Security Level 1		
	Encryption, Mbyte/s	Decryption, Mbyte/s
RC4(IAIK)	52,51	34,66
RC4(SunJCE)	50,01	49,87
RC4(BC)	47,69	29,24
RC4(CryptixCrypto)	46,66	39,88
RC4(JsafeJCE)	40,45	20,98
CAST5(IAIK)	29,53	28,49
Blowfish(CryptixCrypto)	28,74	28,74
Blowfish(IAIK)	28,7	29,74
RC5(IAIK)	28,18	31,33
RC5(BC)	28,16	21,16
CAST5(CryptixCrypto)	24,74	36,67
Blowfish(SunJCE)	23,48	19,08
Blowfish(BC)	21,73	3,22
RC5(JsafeJCE)	20,41	5,07
CAST5(BC)	18,83	21,83
CAST6(BC)	14,13	15,75
RC5(FlexiCore)	5,16	17,14

Symmetric Encryption/Decryption - Security Level 2		
	Encryption, Mbyte/s	Decryption, Mbyte/s
RC4(IAIK)	52,52	52,77
RC4(SunJCE)	49,76	50,26
RC4(BC)	47,75	47,85
RC4(CryptixCrypto)	46,68	46,91
RC4(JsafeJCE)	40,43	40,73
Blowfish(CryptixCrypto)	28,72	36,7
Blowfish(IAIK)	28,64	28,5
RC5(BC)	28,55	29,4
RC5(IAIK)	28,22	34,81
CAST5(IAIK)	25,26	28,8
Blowfish(SunJCE)	23,46	18,66
Blowfish(BC)	21,37	21,5
CAST5(CryptixCrypto)	21,28	30,41
RC5(JsafeJCE)	20,38	20,96
CAST5(BC)	15,73	18,77
CAST6(BC)	14,1	14,15
RC5(FlexiCore)	5,19	5,16

Figure 16: Symmetric Encryption and Decryption(1+2) at operating system Windows Vista

Symmetric Encryption/Decryption - Security Level 3					
	Encryption, Mbyte/s	Decryption, Mbyte/s		Encryption, Mbyte/s	Decryption, Mbyte/s
RC4(IAIK)	52,59	52,76	Rijndael(JsafeJCE)	20,86	18,21
RC4(SunJCE)	49,73	49,88	AES(JsafeJCE)	20,83	53,09
RC4(BC)	47,51	47,93	RC5(JsafeJCE)	20,4	20,94
RC4(CryptixCrypto)	46,64	46,94	Serpent(IAIK)	19,41	17,23
RC4(JsafeJCE)	40,42	40,68	AES(FlexiCore)	17,99	18,48
RC6(IAIK)	34,39	34,95	IDEA(IAIK)	17,84	8,17
Twofish(IAIK)	31,46	20,1	Twofish(FlexiCore)	17,2	14,78
MARS(IAIK)	29,44	24,43	MARS(FlexiCore)	17,19	18,43
AES(IAIK)	28,9	48,13	Serpent(CryptixCrypto)	16,23	11,72
Rijndael(IAIK)	28,81	24,11	CAST5(BC)	15,77	15,7
Blowfish(IAIK)	28,78	28,35	MARS(CryptixCrypto)	15,38	25,27
Blowfish(CryptixCrypto)	28,74	36,82	Serpent(FlexiCore)	14,63	9,56
RC6(CryptixCrypto)	28,74	8,34	CAST6(BC)	14,1	14,18
RC5(BC)	28,57	29,13	Serpent(BC)	12,81	11,15
RC5(IAIK)	28,26	34,84	IDEA(CryptixCrypto)	11,2	7,46
RC6(BC)	28,02	29,31	IDEA(BC)	10,85	6,99
AES(BC)	25,49	46,94	IDEA(FlexiCore)	9,24	5,13
CAST5(IAIK)	25,09	24,43	DESede(IAIK)	8,18	18,53
Rijndael(SunJCE)	25,06	19,99	Twofish(CryptixCrypto)	7,98	20,56
Rijndael(CryptixCrypto)	24,18	21,29	MISTY1(FlexiCore)	7,38	16,13
Blowfish(SunJCE)	22,54	18,28	DESede(BC)	7,01	17,17
AES(SunJCE)	21,63	14,48	DESede(FlexiCore)	5,14	7,07
Blowfish(BC)	21,4	21,93	RC5(FlexiCore)	5,14	5,18
RC6(FlexiCore)	21,37	5,16	DESede(JsafeJCE)	5,03	12,02
Twofish(BC)	21,34	12,92	Rijndael(BC)	3,75	21,38
CAST5(CryptixCrypto)	21,27	25,28			

Figure 17: Symmetric Encryption and Decryption(3) at operating system Windows Vista

33

Symmetric Encryption/Decryption - Security Level 4					
	Encryption, Mbyte/s	Decryption, Mbyte/s		Encryption, Mbyte/s	Decryption, Mbyte/s
RC6(IAIK)	34,33	34,61	AES(BC)	21,07	25,82
Twofish(IAIK)	31,39	31,31	AES(SunJCE)	20,55	17,38
MARS(IAIK)	29,5	29,28	RC5(JsafeJCE)	20,39	20,98
RC6(CryptixCrypto)	28,77	39,89	Serpent(IAIK)	19,37	20,04
Blowfish(CryptixCrypto)	28,7	36,75	AES(JsafeJCE)	17,81	21,33
RC5(BC)	28,66	29,16	Twofish(FlexiCore)	17,46	17,09
Blowfish(IAIK)	28,58	28,39	MARS(FlexiCore)	17,25	16,1
RC5(IAIK)	28,31	34,76	Serpent(CryptixCrypto)	16,21	20,49
RC6(BC)	28,03	29,14	MARS(CryptixCrypto)	15,38	17
AES(IAIK)	23,36	29,79	Serpent(FlexiCore)	14,63	14,75
Blowfish(SunJCE)	23,25	18,91	CAST6(BC)	14,04	14,18
Twofish(BC)	21,48	21,3	Serpent(BC)	12,81	12,86
Blowfish(BC)	21,25	21,91	Twofish(CryptixCrypto)	8,05	8,41
RC6(FlexiCore)	21,23	21,29	RC5(FlexiCore)	5,15	5,17

Figure 18: Symmetric Encryption and Decryption(4) at operating system Windows Vista

Asymmetric Encryption/Decryption		
	Encryption, Kbyte/s	Decryption, Kbyte/s
RSA(SunJCE,1536bit)	224,03	8,22
RSA(FlexiCore,1536bit)	228,32	8,48
RSA(CryptixCrypto,1536bit)	227,47	8,41
RSA(BC,1536bit)	229,41	7,89
RSA(IAIK,1536bit)	226,52	7,74
RSA(JsafeJCE,1536bit)	1118,88	8,60
RSA(SunJCE,2432bit)	149,77	3,68
RSA(FlexiCore,2432bit)	151,00	3,72
RSA(CryptixCrypto,2432bit)	151,55	3,70
RSA(BC,2432bit)	149,74	3,52
RSA(SunJCE,4096bit)	91,63	1,36
RSA(FlexiCore,4096bit)	91,56	1,37
RSA(CryptixCrypto,4096bit)	94,24	1,36
RSA(BC,4096bit)	90,98	1,32
RSA(IAIK,4096bit)	90,67	1,32
RSA(JsafeJCE,4096bit)	514,73	1,44
RSA(SunJCE,6136bit)	61,76	0,63
RSA(FlexiCore,6136bit)	61,50	0,63
RSA(CryptixCrypto,6136bit)	64,07	0,63
RSA(BC,6136bit)	61,48	0,62

Figure 19: Asymmetric Encryption and Decryption at operating system Windows Vista

Signing and Verifying - Security Level 1 (1536 bit key)		
	Signing in Milliseconds	Verifying in Milliseconds
MD5withRSA(BC)	33,97	11,44
MD5withRSA(CryptixCrypto)	27,65	6,92
MD5withRSA(FlexiCore)	29,89	9,36
MD5withRSA(IAIK)	30,59	7,92
MD5withRSA(JsafeJCE)	28,01	7,46
MD5withRSA(SunRsaSign)	27,41	6,94
RIPEMD128withRSA(BC)	37,62	15,39
RIPEMD128withRSA(CryptixCrypto)	40,72	19,78
RIPEMD128withRSA(IAIK)	41,67	19,41
RIPEMD160withRSA(BC)	41,80	19,53
RIPEMD160withRSA(CryptixCrypto)	48,93	28,41
RIPEMD160withRSA(FlexiCore)	37,30	17,01
RIPEMD160withRSA(IAIK)	49,30	26,52
SHA1withRSA(BC)	42,25	19,83
SHA1withRSA(CryptixCrypto)	37,63	16,63
SHA1withRSA(FlexiCore)	34,27	13,69
SHA1withRSA(IAIK)	34,57	11,84
SHA1withRSA(JsafeJCE)	35,12	15,00
SHA1withRSA(SunRsaSign)	37,32	16,52

Figure 20: Signing and Verifying at operating system Windows Vista

Hashing					
	Time in Milliseconds		Time in Milliseconds		Time in Milliseconds
MD5(BC)	10,614705	SHA-1(BC)	19,185192	Tiger(BC)	22,46973
MD5(CryptixCrypto)	7,546405	SHA-1(CryptixCrypto)	13,438384	Tiger(CryptixCrypto)	26,29631
MD5(FlexiCore)	8,627812	SHA-1(FlexiCore)	13,178739	Tiger(FlexiCore)	20,129967
MD5(GNU-CRYPTO)	6,9563	SHA-1(GNU-CRYPTO)	17,672882	Tiger(GNU-CRYPTO)	16,155868
MD5(IAIK)	7,244772	SHA-1(IAIK)	11,341907	Tiger(IAIK)	26,500682
MD5(JsafeJCE)	7,279116	SHA-1(JsafeJCE)	14,663942	Tiger(JsafeJCE)	26,576992
MD5(SunJCE)	6,067737	SHA-1(SunJCE)	16,01745	Tiger(SunJCE)	26,300853
RipeMD160(BC)	18,378999	SHA-256(BC)	26,586172	Whirlpool(BC)	298,857123
RipeMD160(CryptixCrypto)	27,711553	SHA-256(CryptixCrypto)	24,899286	Whirlpool(CryptixCrypto)	89,128958
RipeMD160(FlexiCore)	16,292853	SHA-256(FlexiCore)	30,005392	Whirlpool(FlexiCore)	87,503872
RipeMD160(GNU-CRYPTO)	27,536733	SHA-256(GNU-CRYPTO)	24,344038	Whirlpool(GNU-CRYPTO)	84,925935
RipeMD160(IAIK)	25,916578	SHA-256(IAIK)	20,019456	Whirlpool(IAIK)	89,148117
RipeMD160(JsafeJCE)	26,952845	SHA-256(JsafeJCE)	23,200593	Whirlpool(JsafeJCE)	87,826313
RipeMD160(SunJCE)	27,951685	SHA-256(SunJCE)	25,401871	Whirlpool(SunJCE)	87,87268
RipeMD256(BC)	14,138452	SHA-384(BC)	45,237134		
RipeMD256(CryptixCrypto)	152,977525	SHA-384(CryptixCrypto)	52,187104		
RipeMD256(FlexiCore)	152,060876	SHA-384(FlexiCore)	50,108505		
RipeMD256(GNU-CRYPTO)	153,380642	SHA-384(GNU-CRYPTO)	47,920206		
RipeMD256(IAIK)	152,650172	SHA-384(IAIK)	40,560143		
RipeMD256(JsafeJCE)	156,524303	SHA-384(JsafeJCE)	43,239293		
RipeMD256(SunJCE)	153,610127	SHA-384(SunJCE)	51,44744		
RipeMD320(BC)	18,311195	SHA-512(BC)	46,046969		
RipeMD320(CryptixCrypto)	196,404553	SHA-512(CryptixCrypto)	52,062451		
RipeMD320(FlexiCore)	195,665733	SHA-512(FlexiCore)	50,487592		
RipeMD320(GNU-CRYPTO)	197,572998	SHA-512(GNU-CRYPTO)	48,196024		
RipeMD320(IAIK)	197,444931	SHA-512(IAIK)	40,374766		
RipeMD320(JsafeJCE)	198,422809	SHA-512(JsafeJCE)	43,136351		
RipeMD320(SunJCE)	194,423235	SHA-512(SunJCE)	50,768883		

Figure 21: Hashing at operating system Windows Vista

Creation of a HMac - Duration for 1MByte					
	Time in ms		Time in ms		Time in ms
HMac-MD5(GNU-CRYPTO)	6,04	HMac-SHA1(GNU-CRYPTO)	15,89	HMac-SHA512(CryptixCrypto)	51,94
HMac-MD5(SunJCE)	6,42	HMac-SHA1(CryptixCrypto)	16,11	HMac-SHA512(GNU-CRYPTO)	51,27
HMac-MD5(CryptixCrypto)	6,28	HMac-SHA1(SunJCE)	15,85	HMac-SHA512(BC)	51,11
HMac-MD5(JsafeJCE)	6,43	HMac-SHA1(JsafeJCE)	15,97	HMac-SHA512(IAIK)	51,04
HMac-MD5(IAIK)	6,38	HMac-SHA1(IAIK)	15,96	HMac-SHA512(SunJCE)	51,41
HMac-MD5(FlexiCore)	6,28	HMac-SHA1(BC)	16,13	HMac-SHA512(FlexiCore)	52,24
HMac-MD5(BC)	6,39	HMac-SHA1(FlexiCore)	16,16	HMac-SHA512(JsafeJCE)	51,40
HMac-RipeMD128(SunJCE)	20,11	HMac-SHA256(BC)	24,88	HMac-Tiger(FlexiCore)	22,34
HMac-RipeMD128(FlexiCore)	20,36	HMac-SHA256(JsafeJCE)	25,35	HMac-Tiger(JsafeJCE)	22,56
HMac-RipeMD128(CryptixCrypto)	20,07	HMac-SHA256(SunJCE)	25,03	HMac-Tiger(SunJCE)	22,19
HMac-RipeMD128(JsafeJCE)	19,79	HMac-SHA256(FlexiCore)	25,61	HMac-Tiger(BC)	22,34
HMac-RipeMD128(BC)	20,03	HMac-SHA256(IAIK)	25,21	HMac-Tiger(CryptixCrypto)	22,19
HMac-RipeMD128(IAIK)	20,11	HMac-SHA256(GNU-CRYPTO)	24,72	HMac-Tiger(IAIK)	22,25
HMac-RipeMD128(GNU-CRYPTO)	20,09	HMac-SHA256(CryptixCrypto)	25,76	HMac-Tiger(GNU-CRYPTO)	22,48
HMac-RipeMD160(JsafeJCE)	27,70	HMac-SHA384(SunJCE)	51,52		
HMac-RipeMD160(CryptixCrypto)	27,83	HMac-SHA384(BC)	51,90		
HMac-RipeMD160(BC)	27,57	HMac-SHA384(GNU-CRYPTO)	50,99		
HMac-RipeMD160(IAIK)	27,44	HMac-SHA384(JsafeJCE)	51,40		
HMac-RipeMD160(SunJCE)	28,03	HMac-SHA384(CryptixCrypto)	51,47		
HMac-RipeMD160(GNU-CRYPTO)	27,25	HMac-SHA384(FlexiCore)	51,22		
HMac-RipeMD160(FlexiCore)	27,44	HMac-SHA384(IAIK)	51,20		

Figure 22: HMAC Operation at operating system Windows Vista

LINUX RESULTS

Security Level 1	
	Time in Microseconds
Blowfish(BC)	7126
RC4(IAIK)	7133
CAST5(BC)	7157
Blowfish(GNU-CRYPTO)	7164
CAST6(BC)	7174
Blowfish(CryptixCrypto)	7177
Serpent(BC)	7182
CAST5(GNU-CRYPTO)	7188
RC4(GNU-CRYPTO)	7194
CAST6(GNU-CRYPTO)	7203
Blowfish(IAIK)	7237
CAST5(CryptixCrypto)	7262
Blowfish(SunJCE)	7275
RC4(BC)	7311
RC4(CryptixCrypto)	7365
RC4(SunJCE)	7500
CAST5(IAIK)	7552
Serpent(FlexiCore)	9409
Serpent(GNU-CRYPTO)	13092
RC4(JsafeJCE)	15806

Security Level 2	
	Time in Microseconds
Blowfish(GNU-CRYPTO)	8747
CAST5(CryptixCrypto)	8752
RC4(IAIK)	8757
Blowfish(CryptixCrypto)	8779
Blowfish(BC)	8793
CAST6(GNU-CRYPTO)	8806
Blowfish(IAIK)	8813
CAST5(GNU-CRYPTO)	8813
RC4(GNU-CRYPTO)	8825
CAST6(BC)	8835
CAST5(BC)	8889
RC4(BC)	8911
RC4(CryptixCrypto)	8920
CAST5(IAIK)	8972
Blowfish(SunJCE)	9009
RC4(SunJCE)	9298
RC4(JsafeJCE)	17697

Figure 23: Symmetric Key Generation using Ubuntu: Security Level 1 and 2

Security Level 3			
Time in Microseconds		Time in Microseconds	
Rijndael(FlexiCore)	8890	Serpent(GNU-CRYPTO)	9723
CAST5(BC)	8979	IDEA(BC)	9734
Rijndael(BC)	8991	Twofish(CryptixCrypto)	9738
Rijndael(SunJCE)	9014	RC4(GNU-CRYPTO)	9738
AES(BC)	9024	MARS(CryptixCrypto)	9746
AES(IAIK)	9116	Serpent(BC)	9746
Rijndael(IAIK)	9121	IDEA(CryptixCrypto)	9754
MARS(FlexiCore)	9126	RC6(CryptixCrypto)	9763
AES(FlexiCore)	9137	RC6(GNU-CRYPTO)	9778
MISTY1(FlexiCore)	9158	Blowfish(SunJCE)	9782
AES(SunJCE)	9309	IDEA(IAIK)	9816
MISTY1(GNU-CRYPTO)	9315	Twofish(BC)	9820
Serpent(FlexiCore)	9343	Serpent(IAIK)	9825
IDEA(FlexiCore)	9348	IDEA(GNU-CRYPTO)	9827
Twofish(FlexiCore)	9361	RC4(CryptixCrypto)	9832
Rijndael(GNU-CRYPTO)	9580	CAST5(CryptixCrypto)	9842
AES(GNU-CRYPTO)	9612	MARS(IAIK)	9853
RC6(IAIK)	9643	CAST5(IAIK)	9856
CAST6(GNU-CRYPTO)	9648	Blowfish(CryptixCrypto)	9896
RC6(BC)	9660	RC4(SunJCE)	9952
RC4(IAIK)	9666	DESede(BC)	10037
RC6(FlexiCore)	9673	Serpent(CryptixCrypto)	10058
Blowfish(BC)	9673	Twofish(IAIK)	10098
MARS(GNU-CRYPTO)	9676	DESede(IAIK)	11602
Blowfish(GNU-CRYPTO)	9683	DESede(FlexiCore)	15038
RC4(BC)	9684	Rijndael(JsafeJCE)	17884
CAST5(GNU-CRYPTO)	9690	RC4(JsafeJCE)	18886
Twofish(GNU-CRYPTO)	9690	AES(JsafeJCE)	19936
CAST6(BC)	9712	DESede(GNU-CRYPTO)	23244
Rijndael(CryptixCrypto)	9723	DESede(JsafeJCE)	29875
Blowfish(IAIK)	9723		

Figure 24: Symmetric Key Generation using Ubuntu: Security Level 3

Security Level 4			
Time in Microseconds			Time in Microseconds
AES(BC)	14505	RC6(GNU-CRYPTO)	16035
AES(FlexiCore)	15454	RC6(FlexiCore)	16075
AES(GNU-CRYPTO)	15752	Serpent(FlexiCore)	16106
Blowfish(CryptixCrypto)	15761	Serpent(CryptixCrypto)	16119
RC6(IAIK)	15764	Serpent(GNU-CRYPTO)	16135
Blowfish(BC)	15794	Twofish(GNU-CRYPTO)	16135
Blowfish(GNU-CRYPTO)	15807	Twofish(IAIK)	16151
CAST6(GNU-CRYPTO)	15834	MARS(IAIK)	16158
Blowfish(SunJCE)	15838	AES(IAIK)	16189
CAST6(BC)	15846	Blowfish(IAIK)	16192
MARS(GNU-CRYPTO)	15849	Twofish(CryptixCrypto)	16238
MARS(CryptixCrypto)	15852	Twofish(BC)	16248
RC6(CryptixCrypto)	15855	AES(SunJCE)	16404
RC6(BC)	15872	Serpent(IAIK)	16445
MARS(FlexiCore)	15919	Twofish(FlexiCore)	16878
Serpent(BC)	15999	AES(JsafeJCE)	24253

Figure 25: Symmetric Key Generation using Ubuntu: Security Level 4

Asymmetric Key Generation			
Time in Seconds			Time in Seconds
RSA(SunRsaSign, 1536)	0,69	RSA(SunRsaSign, 4096)	45,33
RSA(FlexiCore, 1536)	0,92	RSA(FlexiCore, 4096)	10,81
RSA(CryptixCrypto, 1536)	0,94	RSA(CryptixCrypto, 4096)	18,95
RSA(BC, 1536)	1,15	RSA(BC, 4096)	27,06
RSA(IAIK, 1536)	0,85	RSA(IAIK, 4096)	29,44
RSA(GNU-CRYPTO, 1536)	3,24	RSA(GNU-CRYPTO, 4096)	32,86
RSA(JsafeJCE, 1536)	1,20	RSA(JsafeJCE, 4096)	26,11
RSA(SunRsaSign, 2432)	2,80	RSA(SunRsaSign, 6136)	229,21
RSA(FlexiCore, 2432)	4,18	RSA(FlexiCore, 6136)	321,32
RSA(CryptixCrypto, 2432)	7,02	RSA(CryptixCrypto, 6136)	445,68
RSA(BC, 2432)	4,51	RSA(BC, 6136)	110,09
RSA(IAIK, 2432)	3,82	RSA(IAIK, 6136)	188,16
RSA(GNU-CRYPTO, 2432)	12,08	RSA(GNU-CRYPTO, 6136)	349,46
		RSA(JsafeJCE, 6136)	193,79

Figure 26: Asymmetric Key Generation using Ubuntu

Security Level 1	
	Time in Microseconds
Blowfish(BC)	7126
RC4(IAIK)	7133
CAST5(BC)	7157
Blowfish(GNU-CRYPTO)	7164
CAST6(BC)	7174
Blowfish(CryptixCrypto)	7177
Serpent(BC)	7182
CAST5(GNU-CRYPTO)	7188
RC4(GNU-CRYPTO)	7194
CAST6(GNU-CRYPTO)	7203
Blowfish(IAIK)	7237
CAST5(CryptixCrypto)	7262
Blowfish(SunJCE)	7275
RC4(BC)	7311
RC4(CryptixCrypto)	7365
RC4(SunJCE)	7500
CAST5(IAIK)	7552
Serpent(FlexiCore)	9409
Serpent(GNU-CRYPTO)	13092
RC4(JsafeJCE)	15806

Security Level 2	
	Time in Microseconds
Blowfish(GNU-CRYPTO)	8747
CAST5(CryptixCrypto)	8752
RC4(IAIK)	8757
Blowfish(CryptixCrypto)	8779
Blowfish(BC)	8793
CAST6(GNU-CRYPTO)	8806
Blowfish(IAIK)	8813
CAST5(GNU-CRYPTO)	8813
RC4(GNU-CRYPTO)	8825
CAST6(BC)	8835
CAST5(BC)	8889
RC4(BC)	8911
RC4(CryptixCrypto)	8920
CAST5(IAIK)	8972
Blowfish(SunJCE)	9009
RC4(SunJCE)	9298
RC4(JsafeJCE)	17697

Figure 27: Symmetric Encryption / Decryption using Ubuntu: Security Level 1 and 2

Security Level 3			
Time in Microseconds		Time in Microseconds	
Rijndael(FlexiCore)	8890	Serpent(GNU-CRYPTO)	9723
CAST5(BC)	8979	IDEA(BC)	9734
Rijndael(BC)	8991	Twofish(CryptixCrypto)	9738
Rijndael(SunJCE)	9014	RC4(GNU-CRYPTO)	9738
AES(BC)	9024	MARS(CryptixCrypto)	9746
AES(IAIK)	9116	Serpent(BC)	9746
Rijndael(IAIK)	9121	IDEA(CryptixCrypto)	9754
MARS(FlexiCore)	9126	RC6(CryptixCrypto)	9763
AES(FlexiCore)	9137	RC6(GNU-CRYPTO)	9778
MISTY1(FlexiCore)	9158	Blowfish(SunJCE)	9782
AES(SunJCE)	9309	IDEA(IAIK)	9816
MISTY1(GNU-CRYPTO)	9315	Twofish(BC)	9820
Serpent(FlexiCore)	9343	Serpent(IAIK)	9825
IDEA(FlexiCore)	9348	IDEA(GNU-CRYPTO)	9827
Twofish(FlexiCore)	9361	RC4(CryptixCrypto)	9832
Rijndael(GNU-CRYPTO)	9580	CAST5(CryptixCrypto)	9842
AES(GNU-CRYPTO)	9612	MARS(IAIK)	9853
RC6(IAIK)	9643	CAST5(IAIK)	9856
CAST6(GNU-CRYPTO)	9648	Blowfish(CryptixCrypto)	9896
RC6(BC)	9660	RC4(SunJCE)	9952
RC4(IAIK)	9666	DESede(BC)	10037
RC6(FlexiCore)	9673	Serpent(CryptixCrypto)	10058
Blowfish(BC)	9673	Twofish(IAIK)	10098
MARS(GNU-CRYPTO)	9676	DESede(IAIK)	11602
Blowfish(GNU-CRYPTO)	9683	DESede(FlexiCore)	15038
RC4(BC)	9684	Rijndael(JsafeJCE)	17884
CAST5(GNU-CRYPTO)	9690	RC4(JsafeJCE)	18886
Twofish(GNU-CRYPTO)	9690	AES(JsafeJCE)	19936
CAST6(BC)	9712	DESede(GNU-CRYPTO)	23244
Rijndael(CryptixCrypto)	9723	DESede(JsafeJCE)	29875
Blowfish(IAIK)	9723		

Figure 28: Symmetric Encryption / Decryption using Ubuntu: Security Level 3

Security Level 4			
Time in Microseconds			Time in Microseconds
AES(BC)	14505	RC6(GNU-CRYPTO)	16035
AES(FlexiCore)	15454	RC6(FlexiCore)	16075
AES(GNU-CRYPTO)	15752	Serpent(FlexiCore)	16106
Blowfish(CryptixCrypto)	15761	Serpent(CryptixCrypto)	16119
RC6(IAIK)	15764	Serpent(GNU-CRYPTO)	16135
Blowfish(BC)	15794	Twofish(GNU-CRYPTO)	16135
Blowfish(GNU-CRYPTO)	15807	Twofish(IAIK)	16151
CAST6(GNU-CRYPTO)	15834	MARS(IAIK)	16158
Blowfish(SunJCE)	15838	AES(IAIK)	16189
CAST6(BC)	15846	Blowfish(IAIK)	16192
MARS(GNU-CRYPTO)	15849	Twofish(CryptixCrypto)	16238
MARS(CryptixCrypto)	15852	Twofish(BC)	16248
RC6(CryptixCrypto)	15855	AES(SunJCE)	16404
RC6(BC)	15872	Serpent(IAIK)	16445
MARS(FlexiCore)	15919	Twofish(FlexiCore)	16878
Serpent(BC)	15999	AES(JsafeJCE)	24253

Figure 29: Symmetric Encryption / Decryption using Ubuntu: Security Level 4

Asymmetric Encryption/Decryption using Ubuntu		
	Encryption, Kbyte/s	Decryption, Kbyte/s
RSA(SunJCE, 1536bit)	297,11	11,15
RSA(CryptixCrypto, 1536bit)	303,59	11,08
RSA(BC, 1536bit)	312,54	10,27
RSA(IAIK, 1536bit)	303,12	10,19
RSA(SunJCE, 2432bit)	207,24	4,87
RSA(CryptixCrypto, 2432bit)	208,17	4,94
RSA(BC, 2432bit)	211,53	4,81
RSA(SunJCE, 4096bit)	130,13	1,96
RSA(CryptixCrypto, 4096bit)	130,46	1,95
RSA(BC, 4096bit)	131,31	1,87
RSA(IAIK, 4096bit)	130,41	1,89
RSA(JsafeJCE, 4096bit)	713,67	2,02
RSA(SunJCE, 6136bit)	88,54	0,90
RSA(CryptixCrypto, 6136bit)	89,19	0,91
RSA(BC, 6136bit)	89,57	0,90

Figure 30: Asymmetric Encryption / Decryption using Ubuntu

Signing and Verifying - Security Level 1 (1536 bit key)		
	Signing in Milliseconds	Verifying in Milliseconds
MD5withRSA(SunRsaSign)	21,862	6,402
MD5withRSA(CryptixCrypto)	21,944	6,357
MD5withRSA(JsafeJCE)	22,455	7,442
MD5withRSA(FlexiCore)	23,283	7,495
MD5withRSA(IAIK)	24,785	8,125
SHA1withRSA(SunRsaSign)	26,621	11,423
SHA1withRSA(CryptixCrypto)	26,770	11,406
SHA1withRSA(JsafeJCE)	27,122	11,198
MD5withRSA(BC)	27,237	10,626
SHA1withRSA(FlexiCore)	27,364	12,282
SHA1withRSA(IAIK)	29,094	12,315
RIPEMD128withRSA(BC)	29,746	13,047
SHA1withRSA(BC)	33,169	17,734
RIPEMD128withRSA(CryptixCrypto)	35,685	20,233
RIPEMD128withRSA(IAIK)	40,730	22,736
RIPEMD160withRSA(CryptixCrypto)	42,028	26,687
RIPEMD160withRSA(IAIK)	42,483	25,863
RIPEMD160withRSA(FlexiCore)	44,626	29,846
RIPEMD160withRSA(BC)	48,556	33,344

Figure 31: Signing and Verifying using Ubuntu

Hashing 1 Megabyte					
	Time in Milliseconds		Time in Milliseconds		Time in Milliseconds
MD5(BC)	98,61	SHA-1(BC)	65,97	Tiger(BC)	70,63
MD5(CryptixCrypto)	131,36	SHA-1(CryptixCrypto)	88,11	Tiger(CryptixCrypto)	55,31
MD5(FlexiCore)	146,61	SHA-1(FlexiCore)	85,51	Tiger(FlexiCore)	65,72
MD5(GNU-CRYPTO)	147,56	SHA-1(GNU-CRYPTO)	81,94	Tiger(GNU-CRYPTO)	75,52
MD5(IAIK)	133,78	SHA-1(IAIK)	83,56	Tiger(IAIK)	56,22
MD5(JsafeJCE)	135,26	SHA-1(JsafeJCE)	89,64	Tiger(JsafeJCE)	54,29
MD5(SunJCE)	175,66	SHA-1(SunJCE)	91,42	Tiger(SunJCE)	53,33
RipeMD160(BC)	31,75	SHA-256(BC)	38,04	Whirlpool(BC)	5,19
RipeMD160(CryptixCrypto)	32,86	SHA-256(CryptixCrypto)	39,29	Whirlpool(CryptixCrypto)	9,77
RipeMD160(FlexiCore)	34,05	SHA-256(FlexiCore)	38,39	Whirlpool(FlexiCore)	9,86
RipeMD160(GNU-CRYPTO)	37,19	SHA-256(GNU-CRYPTO)	42,62	Whirlpool(GNU-CRYPTO)	15,25
RipeMD160(IAIK)	39,87	SHA-256(IAIK)	43,90	Whirlpool(IAIK)	9,82
RipeMD160(JsafeJCE)	35,04	SHA-256(JsafeJCE)	40,81	Whirlpool(JsafeJCE)	9,84
RipeMD160(SunJCE)	38,17	SHA-256(SunJCE)	44,18	Whirlpool(SunJCE)	9,86
RipeMD256(BC)	79,00	SHA-384(BC)	25,64		
RipeMD256(CryptixCrypto)	10,35	SHA-384(CryptixCrypto)	23,87		
RipeMD256(FlexiCore)	10,23	SHA-384(FlexiCore)	22,24		
RipeMD256(GNU-CRYPTO)	10,43	SHA-384(GNU-CRYPTO)	25,05		
RipeMD256(IAIK)	10,26	SHA-384(IAIK)	28,34		
RipeMD256(JsafeJCE)	10,47	SHA-384(JsafeJCE)	25,75		
RipeMD256(SunJCE)	10,35	SHA-384(SunJCE)	24,26		
RipeMD320(BC)	29,22	SHA-512(BC)	25,74		
RipeMD320(CryptixCrypto)	8,18	SHA-512(CryptixCrypto)	23,92		
RipeMD320(FlexiCore)	8,19	SHA-512(FlexiCore)	21,82		
RipeMD320(GNU-CRYPTO)	8,20	SHA-512(GNU-CRYPTO)	24,99		
RipeMD320(IAIK)	8,21	SHA-512(IAIK)	31,46		
RipeMD320(JsafeJCE)	8,17	SHA-512(JsafeJCE)	27,12		
RipeMD320(SunJCE)	8,12	SHA-512(SunJCE)	26,20		

Figure 32: Hashing using Ubuntu

Creation of a HMac - Duration for 1MByte					
	Time in ms		Time in ms		Time in ms
HMac-MD5(BC)	5,68	HMac-SHA1(BC)	10,95	HMac-SHA512(BC)	38,28
HMac-MD5(CryptixCrypto)	5,86	HMac-SHA1(CryptixCrypto)	11,07	HMac-SHA512(CryptixCrypto)	38,82
HMac-MD5(FlexiCore)	5,96	HMac-SHA1(FlexiCore)	11,60	HMac-SHA512(FlexiCore)	39,97
HMac-MD5(GNU-CRYPTO)	5,75	HMac-SHA1(GNU-CRYPTO)	10,94	HMac-SHA512(GNU-CRYPTO)	38,43
HMac-MD5(IAIK)	5,70	HMac-SHA1(IAIK)	10,96	HMac-SHA512(IAIK)	38,43
HMac-MD5(JsafeJCE)	5,71	HMac-SHA1(JsafeJCE)	10,94	HMac-SHA512(JsafeJCE)	38,29
HMac-MD5(SunJCE)	5,70	HMac-SHA1(SunJCE)	11,47	HMac-SHA512(SunJCE)	38,23
HMac-RipeMD128(BC)	19,76	HMac-SHA256(BC)	21,78	HMac-Tiger(BC)	14,31
HMac-RipeMD128(CryptixCrypto)	20,12	HMac-SHA256(CryptixCrypto)	21,83	HMac-Tiger(CryptixCrypto)	14,25
HMac-RipeMD128(FlexiCore)	20,21	HMac-SHA256(FlexiCore)	21,88	HMac-Tiger(FlexiCore)	14,80
HMac-RipeMD128(GNU-CRYPTO)	19,72	HMac-SHA256(GNU-CRYPTO)	21,79	HMac-Tiger(GNU-CRYPTO)	14,24
HMac-RipeMD128(IAIK)	19,79	HMac-SHA256(IAIK)	21,75	HMac-Tiger(IAIK)	14,25
HMac-RipeMD128(JsafeJCE)	19,88	HMac-SHA256(JsafeJCE)	21,74	HMac-Tiger(JsafeJCE)	14,27
HMac-RipeMD128(SunJCE)	20,18	HMac-SHA256(SunJCE)	23,15	HMac-Tiger(SunJCE)	14,83
HMac-RipeMD160(BC)	26,11	HMac-SHA384(BC)	38,39		
HMac-RipeMD160(CryptixCrypto)	26,18	HMac-SHA384(CryptixCrypto)	38,37		
HMac-RipeMD160(FlexiCore)	27,08	HMac-SHA384(FlexiCore)	38,50		
HMac-RipeMD160(GNU-CRYPTO)	26,13	HMac-SHA384(GNU-CRYPTO)	38,27		
HMac-RipeMD160(IAIK)	26,09	HMac-SHA384(IAIK)	38,41		
HMac-RipeMD160(JsafeJCE)	26,06	HMac-SHA384(JsafeJCE)	38,43		
HMac-RipeMD160(SunJCE)	26,67	HMac-SHA384(SunJCE)	39,97		

Figure 33: HMACs using Ubuntu

45

www.ingramcontent.com/pod-product-compliance
Lightning Source LLC
La Vergne TN
LVHW042300060326
832902LV00009B/1162